MW01297870

WordPress

The Ultimate Beginner's Guide!

Andrew Johansen

Table of Contents

Introduction..v

Chapter 1: The Basics of WordPress....................................... 1

Chapter 2: Using the WordPress Service 5

Chapter 3: Establishing Your Own Blog Base 9

Chapter 4: The Dashboard of WordPress.org.....................25

Chapter 5: Writing and Publishing Your Content 33

Chapter 6: Managing Media Files..41

Chapter 7: How to Use WordPress Plugins 47

Conclusion 57

Missing π 8 – 11

Introduction

I want to thank you and congratulate you for purchasing this book…

"WordPress: The Ultimate Beginner's Guide!"

This book will help you master the basics of WordPress. If you're looking for a comprehensive guide for inexperienced WordPress users, this is the perfect book for you.

This book will discuss the basics of WordPress. It will explain the two types of services that you can take advantage of while using this content management system. Then, this book will teach you how to register your own domain name, get a web server, and install the WordPress software. By reading this material, you'll become a skilled WordPress user in no time.

Are you ready to establish your own WordPress blog/site? Do you want to write excellent posts using this service? If so, read this book carefully. It will teach you how to install, manage, and enhance your own WordPress blog/website.

Thanks again for purchasing this book, I hope you enjoy it!

Chapter 1: The Basics of WordPress

WordPress allows you to build websites easily and without spending any money. With this powerful tool, you can share your content to all of the people worldwide without worrying about your marketing budget. As a bonus, WordPress comes as a complete package. It has everything you need to get your own blog or website running.

Because WordPress is free and easy to use, it is the best platform for people who want to set up a private blog or a corporate site. Additionally, it has an active and supportive community of users. You will get the help that you need from other people who use this software.

The Benefits Offered by WordPress

Business owners know that they need a website to facilitate online marketing. However, most of them don't know how to write HTML codes or design webpages. This lack of technical knowledge is the reason why some businesses still don't have a website.

Fortunately, WordPress is here. You won't have to become a skilled programmer because WordPress will write the codes for you. Once you access your WordPress account, your tasks are limited to two:

1. Create your own content.

2. Press a button to share your work with other people.

The WordPress software has the following advantages over similar products:

- Different Options – WordPress comes in two different flavors, namely:

  ○ WordPress.org – This option requires the owner to host his own site. As of today, WordPress allows you to work with your preferred web servers. Businesses use this option to set up their official websites.

  ○ WordPress.com - This is a readymade product for sharing online content. People use it to create personal bogs.

- Simplicity – You can set up your own WordPress site in just a few minutes. Additionally, the software involved in publishing content is intuitive.

- Extensibility – WordPress has a wide range of tools and plugins that you can use for customization purposes. That means you can extend the features of WordPress just by installing some programs.

- Strong Community – This software has a large community composed of loyal users. These people offer online forums, instructive websites, and mailing lists to help other users.

Selecting a Platform

There are many content management systems available today. If you'll run a Google search, you will surely see numerous products and services. This wide range of possible options can be intimidating, especially for people who aren't used to blogging and managing websites. Businessmen and bloggers need to make sure that the platform they use can meet their needs.

With that said, the WordPress service is different because it provides two different types of software, each created to satisfy various needs.

Each WordPress setup has access to certain features, whether it uses self-hosted services or relies on the hosting functionality of WordPress. com. Here are some of the most popular features of WordPress:

- Easy and simple installation
- Powerful blogging capabilities: it allows you to publish online content using an intuitive GUI (i.e. graphical user interface)
- Excellent archiving of posts (through categories)
- Various tools for trackback and comments
- Automated protection against spam (using Akismet)
- Preinstalled gallery feature for your images
- Reliable community
- Limitless quantity of static webpages.
- Different tools for transferring content between different content management systems

The following sections will explain the differences between WordPress. com and WordPress.org. Read this material carefully because it will help you establish the right Wordpress account.

WordPress.com – The Hosted Variant

You can consider WordPress.com as a free hosting service. If you don't want to download, install, and use software from website servers, this is the perfect solution for you. WordPress hosts this service, which means you won't have to worry about downloads, installations, or server settings. The system will take care of the technical stuff for you.

However, it is important to note that WordPress.com has certain restrictions. For example, WordPress.com users cannot use customized themes. Additionally, they cannot alter the core source code or sell advertising services. Despite these limitations, the WordPress.com variant is the ideal option for people who are new to the blogging world.

WordPress.org – The Self-Installed Variant

This version of the WordPress service requires you to download a program and use it on a server. That means you need to lease a web server, unless you own one.

Leasing web servers, usually called "web hosting," isn't free. You need to shell out some cash if you want to use this option. Budget-conscious individuals don't have to worry, however, since web hosting isn't expensive. You can get great website-hosting services for just $5 to $15 per month, based on your hosting needs.

Chapter 2: Using the WordPress Service

This chapter will teach you how to use WordPress. It will give you practical tips and technical ideas. With this approach, you will become an effective WordPress user in no time.

The Different Types of WordPress Users

WordPress users belong to one of these categories:

- Personal – A personal user starts a blog to record his ideas and/ or daily experiences. People will consider you as a personal user if you will use your WordPress site to talk about personal things (e.g. family, pets, hobbies).

- Business – This kind of user creates a blog to market products and/or services. A blog is an effective tool to promote market offerings. Additionally, it offers valuable information to consumers (e.g. tips, recipes, product reviews, etc.).

- Media – People and organizations involved in the media have created blogs to give information regarding different things such as politics.

- Professional – This type has experienced rapid growth in the past few years. A professional blogger is a blogger who gets paid to create blog entries for websites or companies. These days, professional bloggers help online marketers in reaching more potential customers.

- Citizen Journalist – The existence of this group began when people switched to the new type of media. Before, news groups directed the discussion regarding news topics. These days, however, even average citizens can control the conversations about their preferred topics.

The Technologies Used in WordPress

WordPress uses two platforms: MySQL and PHP. MySQL has everything needed in creating a website and publishing online content. That means you can be an effective blogger without programming webpages manually. Additionally, WordPress stores your content in the MySQL database of your hosting service provider.

PHP (i.e. Personal Home Page) is a scripting language that you can use to generate dynamic webpages. Whenever a website visitor accesses a PHP-based webpage, the server works on PHP codes and transmits the data to that person's browser. MySQL, on the other hand, is an open-source RDBMS (i.e. Relational Database Management System) that employs SQL (i.e. Structured Query Language). SQL is a popular computer language used in adding, deleting, accessing, and manipulating data inside databases.

How to Store Your Posts

The WordPress system has a built-in capability to store categorized archives of the user's publishing history. This archiving system is chronological and automated. WordPress employs MySQL and PHP to categorize and organize your content so that you can access them easily.

While creating a post using your WordPress account, you may file that entry under a specific category. This functionality results to a simple and effective archiving system where people can access content written inside a certain category.

How to Interact With the Readers

As a blogger, you surely want to get your readers' feedback. Feedback, also called blog comment, is like incorporating a guestbook into your blog. People may write notes on your site, and you may respond to them. With this functionality, you can expand the thoughts you've presented in your posts.

In the "Dashboard" of your WordPress account, you have full control over the users who can write comments on your posts. Additionally, if a reader leaves a nasty comment, you may easily edit or delete it. If you don't want to interact with your readers, you may disable comments completely.

Chapter 3: Establishing Your Own Blog Base

Before using the WordPress service, you need to establish a "blog base." This task requires more than just getting, installing, and running the WordPress program. You should also specify your own domain (also called "web address") and hosting service provider. It is true that you will download the WordPress program to your computer's hard drive. However, you will install that program to your website host.

In this chapter, you will discover the basics of the technology involved. You will also know how to install WordPress on a website server.

Getting a Domain

This is the first step in creating a WordPress site. Here, you will choose and register a domain name. Domain names are unique website addresses that you will type on your browser to access a site. Some of the most popular domain names are Facebook.com, Google.com, and Twitter.com.

The Extensions

Domain names have extensions such as ".us" and ".com". The domain registrar will ask you to specify the extension that you want to use during the registration process.

Purchasing an extension doesn't affect the other extensions of that domain name. For instance, if you will buy AwesomeBlog.com, other people can still register other extensions for that domain (e.g. AwesomeBlog.org, AwesomeBlog.us, AweSomeBlog.net, etc.). That means if your website will become popular, other people might get a different extension for your domain and steal some website traffic.

Important Note: Domain names are not case-sensitive.

The Registration Process

A domain registrar needs to be certified by ICANN (i.e. Internet Corporation for Assigned Names and Numbers) before it can sell domain names. You will find numerous registrars in the market today. However, some of these companies are notorious in terms of stability and customer service. The list given below will show you the leading domain registrars of today:

- www.register.com
- www.name.com
- www.godaddy.com
- www.networksolutions.com

After choosing a domain registrar, you need to do the following:

1. Select a name for your domain – Your website address is extremely important so you need to choose wisely. For most people, domain names are brands that help in differentiating a blog or website.
2. Make sure that the domain is available – Launch your favorite web browser and visit the website of your chosen domain registrar. Look for a search box and enter the domain that you want to use. In just a few minutes, you'll see whether the name is available or not. Additionally, your screen will show some variants of the domain name, which is helpful if your original entry is no longer available.

3. Important Note: Some registrars offer web-hosting services. That means you can get a domain name and a website host in just one transaction. However, you are not required to sign up for such services.

Searching for a Host

Important Note: You can skip this part if you will sign up for the hosting services of your domain registrar.

Website hosts are groups, businesses, or individuals that offer bandwidth and server space to other people. These hosts usually charge a fee, which means you'll need to shell out more cash. You are extremely lucky if you know a person who will give you bandwidth and server space for free.

Almost all hosts tag WordPress as a third party program. That means you can't ask your host to help you in case you encounter a problem with WordPress (or other third party program). You can simplify things by talking to the customer service of your chosen host before signing up. Ask them whether they support WordPress.

Web hosts typically offer the following services:

- Disk space
- Bandwidth (data transfer limit)
- Email accounts linked to your domain
- FTP (i.e. File Transfer Protocol) access
- Analytic Tools and Site Statistics
- PHP
- MySQL Database

Since you are planning to use the web server for WordPress, you must ensure that your host meets the system requirements of the software involved. These requirements are:

- MySQL 5.0 (or higher)
- PHP 5.2.4 (or higher)

The quickest way to determine whether the service provider meets the system requirements of WordPress is by checking the FAQ page of their website. If the website doesn't have a FAQ webpage, search for the host's contact information and ask your question via email.

Using the File Transfer Protocol

FTP access is a basic element of any hosting package. This protocol allows you to transfer files quickly and easily. As of today, FTP supports two types of file transfers. These are:

- Downloading – You use this type to transfer files from a server to a local machine.

- Uploading – With this type, you will transfer files from a local machine to a web server.

Aside from transferring files, FTP offers the following functionalities:

- See files – You will see the files inside your server as soon as you log in to your FTP account.

- See the "date modified" info of your files – When viewing a file through FTP, you will see the date of its last modification. This information becomes important when you are troubleshooting system problems.

- Check the size of a file – FTP shows the size of your files. With this feature, you can easily manage the storage space of your account.

- Modify files – Most FTP clients offer an interactive GUI (i.e. graphical user interface). That means you can modify your files inside the web server. As you can see, this feature allows you to perform file modifications quickly. You won't have to download and/or upload files just to update the contents of your server.

- Modify access permissions – This functionality, also called Change Mode or CHMOD, controls the kind of run/read/write permissions applied on your server files.

How to Set Up Your FTP Account

Almost all web hosts offer FTP access. Thus, you can simply talk to your host whether this kind of service is available for your account. If that service is available, you can log in to your account and set up FTP. Today, the most popular host management software is cPanel. You will probably see this software while logging in to your account.

Important Note: The instructions and screenshots given below are based on cPanel. If your account uses a different interface, you'll need to get the assistance of your service provider. The ideas regarding FTP usage are the same – you just have to get the specific instructions for using the interface used by the host.

Here are the things you need to do to establish an FTP account:

1. Log in to your account and access cPanel – Usually, you'll go to http://yoursite.com/cpanel to access the cPanel login screen. Type in the login credentials provided by your host and hit OK.

2. Click on "FTP Account" - This will take you to the FTP section of your cPanel account.

3. Check the current FTP account – Some hosting providers create default FTP accounts for their users. If your host created one for you, your screen will show it in the part that says "Account Management." Most of the time, the login credentials of your

hosting account and that of your cPanel account are the same. Here's a screenshot:

4. If this page doesn't have any FTP account, you can create one using the following steps:

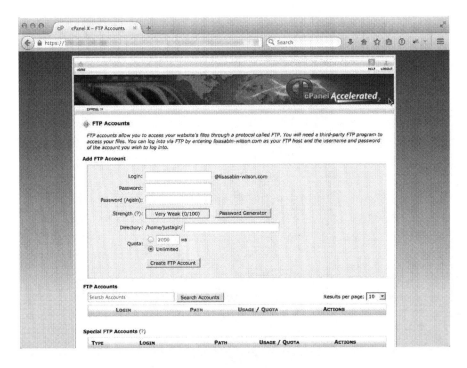

I. Click on the textbox for "Login" and enter the username you want to use. The username that you will get follows this format: login@domainname.com (where "login" is the username you entered and "domainname.com" is the domain name you're working on).

II. Go to the "Password" section and type the password you like to use – You may enter your desired password or allow the system to do it for you. If you choose the latter option, you just have to click on the button that says "Password Generator". Retype the information in the field that says "Password (Again)".

III. Check the Password's strength – The system will evaluate the password's strength and show the result on the screen. The screen may tag your password as "Weak," "Good" or "Strong." Obviously, you need to create a password that belongs to the "Strong" category. If you will use a weak password, hackers might get inside your account and ruin it.

IV. Specify the space limits using the "Quota" section – You are the website owner so you have to make sure that this option is "Unlimited." When creating another user in the same hosting account, you may enter a specific amount (e.g. 100MB) in the appropriate box.

V. Hit the button that says "Create FTP Account" - A new webpage will show up, confirming that the account creation is successful. Aside from this confirmation, the screen will show you the settings of that new account. Copy the information and paste it onto a text editor. You will use this information to access your server through FTP.

VI. Record the settings – You need to record the details of the new account to prevent login and management issues. Here are the details that you should focus on:

a) Username

b) Password

c) The address of the FTP server

d) The space limit

e) The port of the FTP server

Important Note: Usually, FTP servers use 21 as their port. However, your host might set a different one. Just check the confirmation page to see the specific port that you need to use.

Installing the WordPress Software

At this point, you must have completed these tasks:

- Registered your own domain name.

- Acquired hosting services for your site or blog.

- Established the login credentials for your hosting and FTP accounts.

- Obtained a client for transferring files between your local machine and your web server.

Important Note: If you haven't done any of those tasks, you need to go back and reread the earlier sections of this chapter.

Some hosting service providers offer WordPress installers in their software repositories. If your web host offers this feature, you can install the WordPress software quickly and easily. Aside from the installer itself, a web host may also offer a GUI or an installation wizard to simplify the process. Talk to your hosting service provider and ask whether they have this kind of installer. If so, just follow the instructions that come with that program and skip the rest of this chapter.

How to Install the Program Manually

This process is painless, thanks to WordPress' five-minute installation functionality. Keep in mind, however, that the five-minute timeframe only includes the time needed for installing the software itself. This does not include setting up the domain, host, and FTP account. Visit www.wordpress.org/download to start the process. Look for the latest installer and download it.

Important Note: The download page offers two file formats: .tar.gz and .zip. The first option is created for Linux machines. The second one, however, is for Windows computers. Make sure that you are downloading the right format for your computer.

Decompress (i.e. extract) the file after downloading it. Take note of the extract file's location. Now, you've completed the first part of the installation procedure. The next thing you need to do is upload that program to your hosting account and run it there. Ensure that your web server has MySQL before executing the WordPress installer.

How to Set Up MySQL

Here are the things you need to do to set up your own MySQL database:

1. Acces the login page of your cPanel interface and provide the right information (i.e. username and password).

2. Look for the icon that says "MySQL Databases." Click on it.

3. Select a name for your new database and type it in the "Name" field. Make sure that your chosen name is memorable and descriptive. You'll use that information in installing the WordPress program.

4. Hit the button named "Create Database." Your screen will display a message to confirm that the database creation was successful.

5. Go back to the previous webpage and set the login credentials for the new database. Then, hit the link that says "Create User."

6. Return to the previous page once more and highlight the account you just created. Afterward, click on the drop-down menu named "Database" and choose the database you generated earlier. In just a few seconds, your screen will display the "Manage Privileges" page.

7. Since you will be the database administrator, put a check on the box that says "All Privileges." This configuration makes sure that you will be able to do anything you need to do with your database.

8. Save the settings by clicking on the link   named   "Make Changes." The screen will confirm that the account creation process was successful.

9. Refresh the webpage. Go back to the database you've just modified and check its details. It should display the changes you applied.

Uploading the WordPress Installer

Access the location of the extracted WordPress files. Connect to your hosting account through FTP and upload all of the files you see in your current folder. Make sure that the destination of those files is named "root". If you're not sure about the root directory of your FTP account, you may ask your service provider. The screenshot below will serve as a guide:

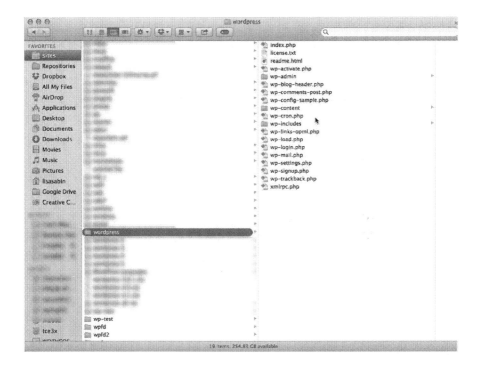

Remember the following principles while uploading files to your server:

- Transfer the extracted files, not the directory itself – Uploading the entire folder might create problems in the installation procedure. Almost all FTP clients allow you to choose multiple files and drag-and-drop them to the web server. Some programs, however, require you to highlight files and hit an "Upload" button.

- Click on the right transfer method – FTP file transfers can take one of these forms: binary and ASCII. Most host systems can detect the transfer method automatically. Knowing the difference between these methods can help you in troubleshooting and fixing problems that may come up in the future.

- ○ The Binary Mode – You should use this mode to transfer image files (e.g. .gif, .jpg, .png, etc.) through FTP.

- ○ The ASCII Mode – This mode works for non-image files (eg. HTML and executable files).

- • Assign the correct file permissions – Permissions inform the server how files must be managed (i.e. whether users can edit them). In general, folders require the "755" permission while PHP files require "644". Most FTP interfaces allow you to view and modify the current permissions of a file. To do this, you just have to check the "Options" page of the FTP interface you're using.

Executing the Installer

This is the last phase of the installation process. Here, you will run the WordPress installer you just uploaded into the database. Here are the things you need to do:

1. Enter the URL given below into the address bar of your browser. Just replace "domainname.com" with your domain name:

http://domainname.com/wp-admin/install.php

If you want to install the WordPress program in a different directory, you need to indicate it in the installation script. For instance, if you want to install the program in a folder named "/private", you have to use the following format:

http://domainname.com/private/wp-admin/install.php

2. Choose your language – If you did everything right, your screen will look like this:

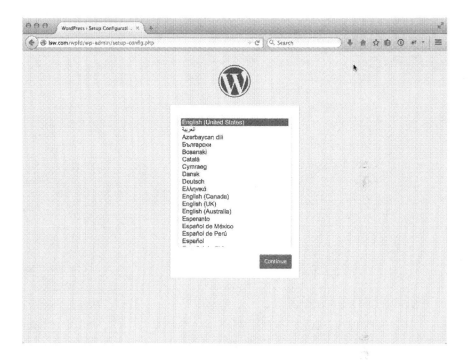

Currently, WordPress supports 47 languages. Choose your preferred language and hit "Continue."

3. Hit the button that says "Let's Go" - Your screen will show a message that welcomes you to the WordPress system. Additionally, it will give you some information about what you should do next.

4. Get the username, password, and database name you stored previously. Then, enter the information in the appropriate fields. Here's another screenshot:

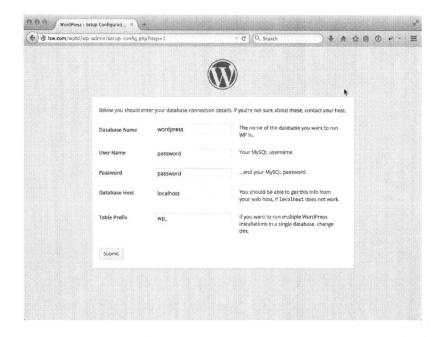

5. Hit the button that says "Submit" once you have typed all the needed data. Your screen will tell you that everything is set and that you are ready to install the WordPress software.

6. Look for the "Run" button to begin the installation procedure. The screen will show you another message. This time, it will introduce you to the five-minute installation process offered by WordPress.

7. Provide the information you want to use with the WordPress system. Here are the details that you need to provide:

    i. The Site Title – You should enter the title you want to assign for your site/blog. Don't worry if you're not yet sure about the title you like to use. You can change this detail later.

ii. The Username – You will use this information to access your WordPress account. The default username of WordPress accounts is "admin." Your account will work as normal even if you won't change that detail. However, you can greatly improve your account's security by changing the username.

iii. The Password – This section involves two boxes. Type the password you want to use in the first box. Then, retype it in the second one. The WordPress system will notify you if the passwords you entered don't match. If you won't set a password, the system will generate one for you.

iv. Your Email Address – You have to provide an email address so that WordPress can update you regarding your account. Just like the site title, you can change this detail in the future.

v. Let search engines index your website – You will see a checkbox that asks whether you want search engines (e.g. Google) to index your online content and include it in their search results. Put a check on this box if you want to share your content with the world. If you want to use the site as a private journal, however, make sure that this box is unchecked.

8. Click on the button that says "Install WordPress" - The WordPress program will run and prepare the database for your online content. Your screen will display your login information – read it and make sure that everything is correct. After hitting the installation button, WordPress will send you an email containing your login credentials and a URL. You'll need that

information in case you need to go away while the installation process is running.

9. Access the WordPress system – The screen will show you a button named "Log In." Click on it to continue the process. If this button is not available, you can access the right webpage by typing: http://domainname.com/wp-login.php in your browser's address bar. If your screen shows the login page of WordPress, you can be sure that the installation process was successful.

Chapter 4: The Dashboard of WordPress.org

Once you have installed WordPress.org, you will be able to use its software. In this chapter, you will learn how to use the system's Dashboard in setting up your new site.

You will spend a lot of time in your Dashboard. This part of WordPress is responsible for doing all the good stuff within your website. Using the Dashboard, you will be able to establish your site and customize it according to your needs.

Getting comfortable with the Dashboard helps you to become successful in the WordPress universe. Be prepared to change your password many times throughout your site's existence. While studying the options and settings discussed in this chapter, remember that you can change almost everything in the Dashboard. That means you can alter the configuration of your website anytime you want.

Accessing the Dashboard

You need to access the Dashboard before making changes on your account and website. Here are the steps you need to take when logging in to your WordPress Dashboard:

1. Launch a web browser and enter the login URL of your WordPpress account. The format that you should use is: http:// www.domainname.com/wp-login.php.

2. Type your login credentials in the appropriate boxes. If you can't remember your password, you just have to click on the link that says "Lost Your Password?" Then, hit the "Get a New Password" button. The WordPress system will reset your

password and send you an email regarding the changes.

3. If you like WordPress to place a cookie inside your web browser, put a check on the "Remember Me" box. This cookie informs WordPress to remember the login formation you entered. Thus, next time you need to access your account, you won't have to type your account credentials anymore.

4. Hit "Log In" - This is the final part of the login procedure. Assuming that you entered the right information, your screen should show you the Dashboard of your WordPress account.

Working with the Dashboard

Some people think of the Dashboard as the control panel of their WordPress account. That's because the Dashboard contains the settings and options that you can use to manage your website. Additionally, it offers links and pages that help you to learn more about your account. Here's what the WordPress Dashboard looks like:

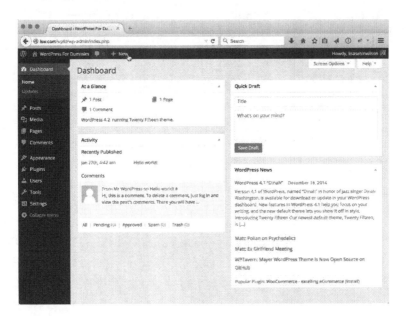

Wordpress allows you to customize your Dashboard by rearranging its modules. You may open (expand) or close (collapse) a module by clicking on the small arrow near its title. This is one of the best features of the WordPress Dashboard. Here, you can minimize the modules that you don't need. Managing your account will be simpler and easier since irrelevant options will stay hidden.

Important Note: WordPress remembers the setup of your Dashboard. That means you won't have to make the changes each time you log in.

If you'll look at the left side of your screen, you will see the navigation options of your Dashboard. Just click on the "Dashboard" button whenever you need to return to the main webpage of the Dashboard.
The At a Glance Module

This module shows some information about what's happening in your site, at this very moment. If you'll open it, you will see the following details:

- The total number of your posts – This part shows the number of active posts in your blog or website. The number is clickable – clicking on it will take you to another webpage where you can edit your posts.

- The total number of your webpages – This detail shows the number of pages inside your blog. It will change automatically as soon as you add/delete a webpage. The number is clickable – click on it if you want to edit the webpages of your site.

- The total number of readers' comments – With this part, you'll know the specific number of comments written on your blog/ website. Just like the previous two, the number of this section is also clickable. Click on the number if you want to control the comments within your site.

The Activity Module

This module consists of the following areas:

- Recently Published – Check this area if you want to view your latest posts. This part of the Dashboard will show the title of your new posts as well as their date of publication. Keep in mind that each entry is a live URL. Clicking on a post will take you to the "Edit Post" section of the Dashboard.

- Recent Comments – This area shows up to five comments.

- The authors of the comments – In this area, you'll find the person who left each comment. This will also show the avatar of the user if he/she has one; otherwise, the screen will show the default image.

- Links to the posts where the comments were wrote on – You'll find a link beside the commenter's username. Click on that link if you want to check the post he/she commented on.

- Excerpts of the comments – This module will also show you the snippets of the latest comments. That means you can see what the comments are about without checking the posts directly.

The Quick Draft Module

This module is a powerful tool that lets you write, publish, and store posts straight from the Dashboard. If you've just installed your WordPress system, the "Drafts" section of "Quick Draft" won't be available. That's because you haven't stored any post as a draft. As you continue using your WordPress account, however, you will surely save drafts of your website posts.

By default, your Dashboard will show five drafts. Each entry has a title and the date of its last modification. Click on the title to access the "Edit Post" webpage where you can read and modify the saved post. You'l learn more about writing and editing posts in a later chapter.

Managing Your Profile

The default settings of the Dashboard work for any type of account. However, if you want to personalize your profile and own your WordPress account completely, WordPress got you covered. You just have to click on the link that says "Your Profile" to make the necessary modifications.
WordPress allows you to change the following:

- Personal Settings – Here, you can change some options for your site. These options are:

  - Visual Editor – You can use this section to enable the "Visual Editor" while you are writing posts. This editor provides you with editing and formatting options available in the "Write Post" webpage.

  - Color Scheme – This section allows you to adjust the colors of your WordPress Dashboard. By default, the color of the Dashboard is gray and black. WordPress offers different color schemes (e.g. Coffee, Light, Ectoplasm, etc.). Here's a screenshot of the Color Scheme section:

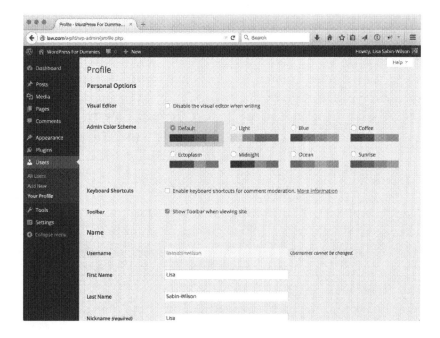

○ Keyboard Shortcuts – In this section, you can set the keyboard shortcuts to be used for comment management.

○ Toolbar – The WordPress Toolbar appears at the upper part of the WordPress site. However, only the active user can see it (i.e. ordinary readers won't see this section). The toolbar of WordPress contains useful links that you can use to reach various parts of your site quickly.

• Name – Use this section to provide your personal data (e.g. nickname, last name, first name, etc.) and set how the system will show your name to other people. Enter the information in the appropriate boxes. Then, click on the drop-down menu and choose the "display name" you want to use.

- Contact Information – This section allows you to set your website URL and email address. WordPress will share the said information with other users so they can contact you easily. Keep in mind that only the email address is required here. You don't have to provide a URL if you don't want to.

- About Yourself – Here, you can set the password for your account and create a short bio. Some themes show the author's bio, so you need to be unique and creative when writing your short biography.

Chapter 5: Writing and Publishing Your Content

The WordPress system is an excellent sharing tool, especially if you will utilize all of the options available to you. Since you have set the basics of your account in the previous chapter, it's time to write and share your online content.

In this chapter, you'll find practical tips and technical ideas that can help you create great posts. Read this material carefully if you want your blog/site to get a lot of readers.

How to Stay on Topic

You can use the "category" feature of WordPress to keep your blog or website organized. This feature helps you in filing posts under specific subjects. The system improves the experience of readers by displaying posts according to the categories assigned by the author. Readers may click on the category that interests them to view the entries you wrote about that topic.

You must remember that the categories you assigned appear in different parts of the website. Here are some examples:

- The body of a post – Most themes in WordPress display the category where each post belongs to. You'll see this detail right beside the title of a post. Additionally, readers may click on any category to find the posts you wrote regarding that topic.

- The sidebar – WordPress allows you to show your categories in the sidebar of your site.

Important Note: You can also create subcategories to refine your topics further. You just have to access your Dashboard and click on the link that says "Manage Categories." The option to create and modify subcategories will show up on your screen.

How to Change a Category's Name

After the installation process, WordPress will place a category in your account named "Uncategorized." You can change its name to something else. Keep in mind that this category will "catch" all of your uncategorized posts (even after renaming it). Here are the steps you need to follow when changing the name of your category:

1. Log in to your account and access the "Posts" menu. Your screen will display the "Categories" webpage, which contains the tools that you can use to edit category names.

2. Click on the name of the category you want to modify. If you want to rename "Uncategorized", click on that word to access the Edit webpage.

3. Enter the name you want to use in the appropriate field.

4. Click on the dropdown menu named "Parent" and select a category. Make sure that this option is set to "None" if you don't want to set the current category as a subcategory.

5. Click on the button that says, "Update." The system will save the information you provided and reload the page. In just a few seconds, your screen will reflect the recent changes.

How to Create a New Category

You'll need to create more categories as you continue using your WordPress account. Obviously, categories help you in keeping your website organized. WordPress doesn't have limits regarding categories. That means you can create as many categories as you need.

To create a new category, you should do the following:

1. Go to your Dashboard and hit the "Categories" button. This action will open the "Categories" page.

2. Look at the left-hand side of the page and click on "Add New Category." Your screen will look like this:

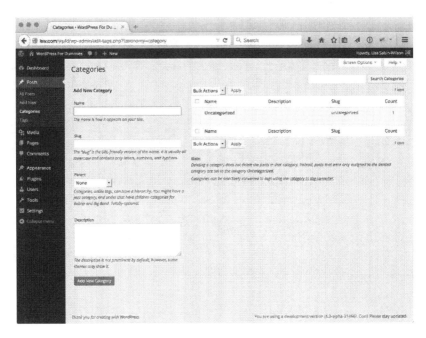

3. Enter the name you want to use for the new category.

4. Select the parent category from the dropdown menu. If you want to this category to be a top-level (or main) category, set the option to "None."

5. Hit the button that says "Add New Category." Congratulations! You'll be able to use the new category for your next posts. Repeat this procedure to create more categories for your account.

How to Delete a Category

Deleting a category is easy and simple. You just have to point your mouse on the category you need to remove. Then, hit the "Delete" option that will appear under the category's name.

Important Note: This process doesn't erase the links and posts within the category. Rather, it will transfer all of those links and posts to the default category (which was named "Uncategorized").

Creating Your First Post

Now, you will be writing your first entry in the WordPress system. The subject you'll create posts about as well as the techniques that you'll use depend on you. In this part of the book, you'll learn how to write posts using WordPress.

How to Compose a Blog Post

Writing a post is similar to creating an email: you need to assign a title, write a message, and hit a link/button to send your message.

Important Note: WordPress allows you to move or collapse the modules inside the Add Post webpage according to your preferences. The only part of the page that you can't control is the post and title box (i.e. the part where you will write the post).

Here are the things you need to do to create a post:

1. Access your Dashboard, click on "Posts," and hit "Add New." Your screen will show you this:

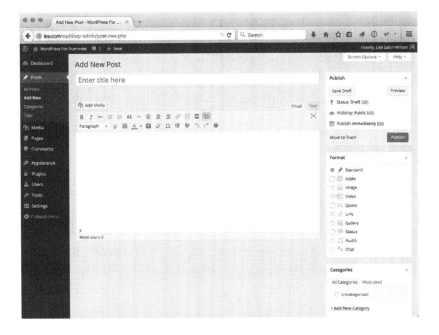

2. Enter the title of the post in the appropriate field.

3. Write the post's content in the large textbox. In WordPress, you can format your work using the "Visual Editor." You'll learn about that feature later.

4. Hit "Save Draft" inside the "Publish" section. By default, "Publish" is located at the page's right-hand side. By hitting the said button, you're telling the system to save your content without sharing it with the world.

The Visual Editor

This is the default tool that you will use to create blog posts. With this tool, WordPress offers formatting options to users. Instead of embedding HTML codes in each of your posts, you can just write your content, highlight the words you need to modify, and hit the buttons found at the upper part of your screen. The screenshot given above shows the visual editor of WordPress.

Important Note: This tool offers formatting options similar to a typical word processing application (e.g. Microsoft Word).

How to Add Sounds, Videos, and Pictures to Your Posts

While working with the Visual Editor, you will surely see the section called "Add Media." This section contains icons that help you in inserting photos, galleries, audio, and video files to your content. These icons are self-explanatory – you won't have any problems using them when writing a post.

How to Refine Your Posts

After writing your post, you may select some bonus options before sharing it with other people. WordPress will apply these settings to the content you're working on. By default, these options are located near the bottom of your screen. You can click on an option's name to expand and use it.

If your screen doesn't show any of these options, that means you need to enable them in the "Screen" page. Click on the "Screen Options"

link at the upper part of the Add Post page and activate the modules that you want to use.

Publishing Your Content

You finished assigning a title to your post and wrote its content. Maybe you also added media files to your post and configured its tags, options, and categories. Now, you are ready to publish your post so other people can see it.

The WordPress system offers three choices for storing or sharing your content once you've completed it. If you'll look at the right-hand side of the Add Post page, you will find the module called "Publish." Click on the module's title to expand it. Here are some of the settings that you will see inside this module:

- Preview – Hitting this button will open a new browser window. The new window will show you how the post will appear once you have published it. Using this button won't publish the post yet. Thus, you should use this option to make sure that your blog appears as planned.

- Save Draft – This option allows you to store posts as drafts. The "Edit" page will reload all of the options and contents of your posts. You may continue working on them at a later date. Once you're ready to complete your posts, hit "Edit" in the "Posts" options.

- Status – You can access the settings of this option by hitting the "Edit" link. Upon clicking "Edit," you will see a dropdown menu that offers two choices. The choices are:

  - Draft – Choose this option to save the content without publishing it.

- ◦ Pending Review – With this option, you can send the current post to a group of drafts right beside the "Pending Review" section. Site contributors use this option to submit their work to the administrator.

- Publish – Click on this button if you don't want to waste your time anymore. The "Publish" option will ignore the rest of the publishing procedure and send the post straight to your site.

How to Edit a Post

In WordPress, you have the freedom to edit your posts anytime you want. That means you can correct mistakes (e.g. grammatical errors) without rewriting the entire post. Follow these steps to polish your WordPress entries:

1. Click on "All Posts" and search for the post that you need to work on. After doing this, your screen will show the twenty of your latest WordPress posts. Click on the "All Dates" menu at the upper part of the screen to filter the list. This way, you can easily find the post you're interested in.

2. Access the "Edit" page by hitting the title of the post.

   Important Note: If you just want to edit the options of a post, you don't have to visit the actual editing page. Just click on the link that says "Quick Edit." The resulting page allows you to modify the post's title, timestamp, status, categories, etc.

3. Make the necessary changes and hit "Update." The system will refresh your window and reflect the latest changes.

Chapter 6: Managing Media Files

Inserting photos and images to your WordPress posts can greatly enhance your blog/website. Through these files, you can share feelings and information that plain text cannot hope to express. This statement also applies to sound and video files. An audio file allows you to "converse" with your readers and give a sense of personality to your website. Video files, on the other hand, helps you in entertaining guests.

This chapter will teach you how to boost your site's effectiveness through media files. Read this material carefully if you want to master the WordPress system.

How to Insert Images

The built-in image uploader of WordPress makes insertion of images easy and simple. You may try it now by accessing the "Add Post" page and hitting the "Add Media" option. The screen will launch a new window and ask you to specify the file/s you want to add. In WordPress, you may use files that you have stored in your computer or those that are available online. Your screen will look like this:

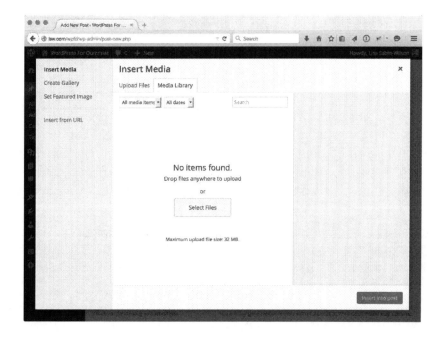

How to Add an Image from an Online Source

Here are the things you need to do when adding an "online" file to your post:

1. Access the window named "Insert Media" and hit "Insert." This action will activate the URL window.

2. Enter the website address of the image you want to add into the "URL" field. Provide the entire address, including the "www" and "http://" portions. Getting the exact URL of an image is easy. Just right-click on the image and choose "Properties" from the resulting options.

3. Enter the word/s you like to display for the selected image.

4. Complete the process by hitting the button that says "Insert into Post."

How to Add an Image from your Computer

1. Click on "Add Media" and "Select Files." Your screen will display a small window, asking you to choose the file/s you want to upload.

2. Choose the photo/s you like to use and hit "Open." The WordPress system will transfer the selected images to the web server. You'll see a small bar on the screen that shows the progress of the upload.

3. Alter the information for the photo/s by through the "Options" section. You'll see this section at the right-hand side of the current window. Here are some of the options that you'll see on your screen:

   I. Title – This will serve as the name of your image.

   II. Description – Use this field to describe your uploaded file.

   III. Alignment – This section offers four choices: Left, None, Right and Center.

4. Click on the button named "Insert into Post."

How to Align Your Images

WordPress allows you to specify the alignment of your uploaded images. However, some WordPress themes don't support alignment styles (e.g. Center, Left, None, etc.) in their stylesheet. For instance, if you'll choose the "Left" alignment but your images don't follow the said setting, you must change the stylesheet of your theme. Here are the things you need to do to get that done:

1. Access the Appearance section and hit "Editor." Your screen will show you the "Edit Themes" webpage. It contains all of the files related to your current theme.

2. Hit the template named "Stylesheet." The textbox at the left-hand side of the screen will show you the .css file.

3. Apply the necessary changes. The window will show you the styles that you can add to the file.

How to Insert a Video File

WordPress offers simple upload processes for video files. That means you can add videos into your posts without worrying about technical difficulties. To add a video to your post, follow these steps:

For Online Videos (e.g. YouTube files)

1. Go to the "Add Media" page and hit the link that says "Insert from URL."

2. Enter the complete URL of the video. Most video providers (e.g. YouTube) offers direct links for their video files. You may just "copy-paste" the information into the appropriate field.

3. Specify the video's title using the "Title" textbox. This step is completely optional: the videos will play as normal even if you don't assign their title. However, it's always a good idea to give a title to each of your videos. This way, you can inform your visitors regarding the content of each material.

4. Hit the button that says "Insert into Post."

You may add a link that your readers can click on to watch the video using a different website. Additionally, WordPress has a cool functionality named "Auto-Embed." Auto-Embed detects the URLs you include in your post and embeds videos automatically, hence the name. This is a built-in functionality – you don't have to change anything in your account to activate it.

For Videos in Your Local Computer

1. Access the "Add" page or the "Edit" page and hit the icon named "Add Media."

2. Choose the video you want to use and double-click on it. Alternatively, you may highlight the file and click on the "Open" button. The system will upload the file you selected. The process might be short or long, depending on your internet speed and the file's size. You'll see a new window once WordPress has completed uploading the video.

3. Provide a title for the video.

4. Add a caption for your video.

5. Describe the newly uploaded file using the "Description" field.

6. Click on the button named "Insert into Post."

How to Insert an Audio File

In WordPress, you can insert different audio files into your posts. That means you can enhance posts by inserting your voice recordings or some music files. Keep in mind that sounds can add "personality" into your website. Additionally, you can use the "Upload Audio" functionality of WordPress to share your audio files with other people. A website guest may download the songs you inserted or play them online.

Here are the things you need to do to upload a sound file:

1. Click on the button named "Select Files."

2. Select the audio file you need to upload and hit "Open." Double-clicking on the file works too. In a few seconds, your screen will display a progress indicator. The entire process might take several minutes, depending on the file you're working on and your internet connection.

3. Wait for the upload to complete. Then, enter the title, caption, and description of the sound file.

4. Click on "Insert into Post."

Important Note: WordPress offers a wide range of audio management plugins. You can use these plugins to improve the effectiveness of the uploader and assist you in managing your files. You'll learn more about WordPress plugins in the next chapter.

Chapter 7: How to Use WordPress Plugins

According to many users, trying out the numerous plugins offered by WordPress is an important part of blog/website development. You may think of a WordPress plugin as an awesome custom rim that you can use on your car. Plugins are optional. However, just like custom car accessories, they can make your blog/website better than others.

This chapter will explain the basics of plugins. After reading this material, you will know how to search for them and use them. Additionally, you will discover how they can add uniqueness to your website.

Plugins – The Basics

Plugins are small programs that, once added to a site, communicates with the internal program to improve the site's functionality. A plugin doesn't belong to a program's core structure, nor can it work as a standalone product. To use a plugin, you need to install it onto a website first.

The WordPress system offers numerous plugins, most of which are free. Discussing each plugin is extremely impractical so we'll focus on the most important ones:

- Email Notification – As its name implies, this plugin allows readers to sign up for email notifications. The system will send emails to your "followers" each time you update your website.

- Stats – This plugin helps you in analyzing the source/s of your website traffic. It will identify your most popular posts as well as your site's overall traffic. You can filter the results on a yearly, monthly, or daily basis.

The Plugins Section

Before installing any plugin on your website, you need to visit the Plugins section of your Dashboard and learn how to control installed plugins. You can access the Plugins area by clicking on "Plugins" and "Installed Plugins." Here's a screenshot:

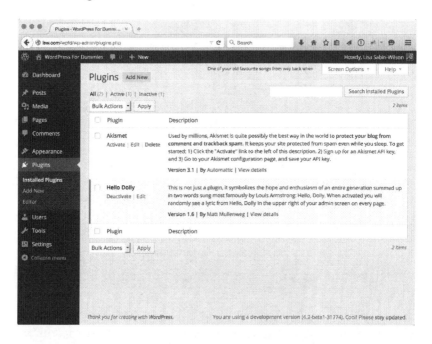

You need to access this page to manage the plugins you installed on your website. If you will visit this webpage for the first time, it will show you all of the plugins present on your site. However, you can filter the plugins based on different criteria (e.g. drop-ins, active, must use, etc.).

Important Note: WordPress allows "mass management" when it comes to plugins. For instance, you may deactivate all of your site's plugins just by checking the box for each plugin and clicking on "Deactivate." Then you can finalize the changes by hitting "Apply."

How to Update a Plugin

Just like any software, plugins are prone to bugs and vulnerabilities. Hackers might exploit these vulnerabilities to access your account. Because of this, plugin developers improve their products and submit updates on a regular basis. That means you need to update all of your plugins to keep your site secure. However, visiting the developer's site daily just to check for updates can be time-consuming.

Well, you don't have to worry: WordPress got you covered. The system will inform you regarding the updates available for your plugins. Thus, keeping your account secure is as simple as waiting for short messages on your screen.

The quickest way to search for updates is by opening the Dashboard menu and clicking on "Updates." This option will show you the total number of updates available to your account. Here's a screenshot:

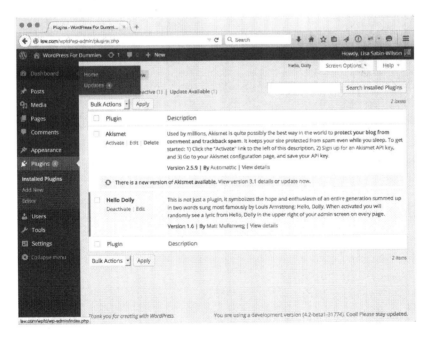

Once you click on the Updates link, you will be redirected to a page where you can update your plugins. Choose the plugins that you want to work on and hit "Update Now." The system will make the necessary changes for you. It will get the updated files from the software repository, upload them to your directory, remove the outdated plugins, and activate the new ones.

The Pre-Installed Plugins

Currently, WordPress comes with two preinstalled plugins. These plugins are:

- Hello Dolly – You can use this plugin to add more fun to your website. According to WordPress experts, Hello Dolly doesn't play an important role in site management.

- Akismet – This is one of the most essential plugins currently available. You'll learn more about it in the next section.

How to Use Akismet

Many people consider Akismet as the primary plugin in WordPress and that blogs are incomplete if they don't have it. This belief is supported by the fact that WordPress has included Akismet in its installation files. Akismet helps you to prevent spam trackbacks and comments. Here are the things you need to do to activate this plugin:

1. Access the "Plugins" webpage, search for Akismet, and click on the link that says "Activate." Your screen will look like this:

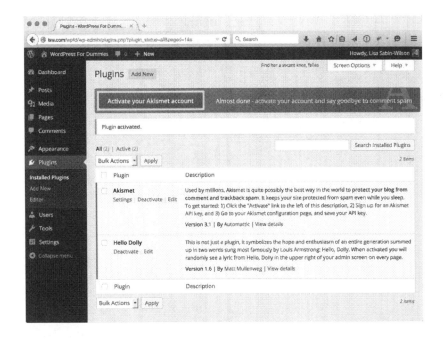

2. Click on the blue button at the top of your screen.

3. Look for the button named "Get Your API Key" and click on it. This action will launch a new window and show you the website of Akismet.

4. Get your API key for Akismet. The screen will ask you to sign in using your WordPress account credentials. Enter the required information and hit "OK."

5. Type your website's URL and choose a payment plan. As of now, you have three options to choose from:

   i. Personal – This plan is for site individuals who use a small WordPress-powered site. You are not required to pay for anything since you will use the plugin for personal purposes. However, you may donate up to $48 each your to support Akismet's campaign against spam.

ii. Business – This option costs $5 per month. It is ideal for those who have a small business WordPress-based website.

iii. Enterprise – This plan is for people and organizations who own different WordPress-powered sites. It costs $50 per month. However, this option is a good one because it can protect all of your WordPress sites from spammers.

6. Copy your API key. Make a payment if necessary.

7. Go back to your Dashboard, click on "Settings" and "Akismet."

8. Paste your API key onto the appropriate field and hit the button named "Use This Key."

Working with Plugins

In this part of the book, you will learn how to install plugins to your blog using the preinstalled plugin feature of WordPress.

Important Note: The process described here works only for the plugins officially supported by WordPress. You'll learn how to install "unsupported" plugins later.

Follow these steps to install a plugin on your WordPress site:

1. Access the menu named "Plugins" and hit "Add New." Your screen will open a new window and show you the official plugins directory of WordPress.

2. Look for a plugin that interests you. The directory you're looking at has a built-in search engine. You can enter keywords to speed up your search. If you want to use a plugin that integrates Twitter into your site, you should type "Twitter" in the search box and hit Enter.

3. Click on the plugin and hit "More Details." This step helps you to learn more about the plugin. You should know how a plugin works before installing it onto your site. The last thing you want to do is waste your time on installing and uninstalling a plugin that doesn't match your website's needs.

4. Click on the button that says "Install Now." Your screen will show you the Plugin Installation webpage.

How to Install a Plugin Manually

This section will teach you how to download, unpack, upload, and activate a plugin manually.

Important Note: To help you understand this process, the author will focus on the Twitter plugin.

Here are the steps you need to follow:

1. Access the plugin directory of WordPress. Type http://wordpress. org/plugins in your browser's address bar.

2. Run a search for Twitter in the built-in engine of WordPress.

3. Scan the results page and look for the correct entry. Then, click the plugin's name. The screen will show you detailed information regarding the plugin. Here's a screenshot:

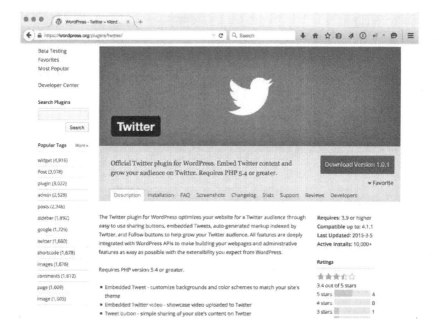

4. Choose the version of the plugin that you want to use and hit "Download." Remember the directory you used in downloading the software. The specific steps in downloading files differ from browser to browser.

5. Access the downloaded file and unzip it using any decompression program.

6. Go back to your Dashboard. Then, click on "Plugins" and "And New."

7. Look at the top section of the webpage and click on "Upload Plugin." Your screen will show you a dialog box that accepts zip files.

8. Click on "Choose File," locate the plugin you want to install, and hit "Open."

9. Hit the button that says "Install Now." The system will upload the file into the "plugins" directory of your server. Then, it will unpack and install the file into your site. The process is automatic. You just have to wait for your screen to show a confirmation regarding the successful (hopefully) installation of the new program.

Conclusion

Congratulations for finishing this book, I hope it was able to teach you the basics of the WordPress content management system.

The next step is to continue writing posts in your blog or website.

Finally, if you enjoyed this book, please take the time to share your thoughts and post a positive review on Amazon. It'd be greatly appreciated!

Thank you and good luck!

Made in the USA
Middletown, DE
17 June 2016